SHIRE NATUR

GW01003632

THE PHEASANT

P. A. ROBERTSON

CONTENTS

Cover: *Territorial cock pheasant with enlarged wattles and ear tufts guarding a hen while she feeds.*

Series editors: Jim Flegg and Chris Humphries.

Copyright © 1988 by P. A. Robertson. First published 1988.
Number 29 in the Shire Natural History series. ISBN 0 85263 950 3.

Set in 9 point Times roman and printed in Great Britain by C. I. Thomas & Sons (Haverfordwest) Ltd, Press Buildings, Merlins Bridge, Haverfordwest, Dyfed.

Pheasants of the world

SPECIES

The Common Pheasant is a member of the order Galliformes, a group with a worldwide distribution but concentrated in the Himalayas, China and south-east Asia. As well as the different species of pheasant, the Galliformes also includes such other groups as the partridges, quail, grouse, turkeys and guinea-fowl.

The Common Pheasant is one of the 47 different pheasant species, the other 46 often being referred to as exotic, fancy or cage pheasants. These other species include the peacocks, tragopans, junglefowl and the argus, monal, eared, kalij, ruffed and long-tailed pheasants.

The peacocks are the largest of the pheasants and are easily recognised by the magnificent tail feathers of the males. The males of the less well known argus pheasants also carry extravagant feathers used in display, but in this case it is the wing feathers. As well as the true peacocks, there is also another group of birds known as the peacock pheasants. These are small, secretive birds with grey or brown plumages but marked with shimmering metallic eyes or ocelli similar to those of the true peacocks whose name they carry. The monal pheasants live in high mountain ranges in Asia; they are superbly coloured, the males sporting metallic blue, gold and green feathers. The tragopans are secretive birds of the forest. The males carry extravagant 'bibs' under their chins which they inflate during courtship and their flank feathers are marked with vivid eye spots.

The junglefowl are the ancestors of the domestic chicken and the similarities can be clearly seen. Of all birds, the junglefowl have probably had the closest relationship with man. The eared pheasants are large birds with prominent tufts of feathers, starting below the eye and curling up to form prominent 'ears'. The kalij pheasants are another group, with laterally compressed tails and brightly coloured wattles.

The true and long-tailed pheasants include the Common Pheasant and other similar species. The Reeves Pheasant is a member of this group and has one of the largest tails of any bird, individual feathers reaching up to 2 metres (6½ feet) in length.

Lastly, the ruffed pheasants include only two species, the Gold and Lady Amherst's Pheasants (*Chrysolophus pictus* and *C. amherstiae* respectively). Both species originated in China but have been successfully introduced to Britain. They live in extensive post-thicket stage coniferous plantations or under areas of mature yew. Neither is found at more than a handful of sites, they are rarely seen and their brilliant, multicoloured plumages do not allow them to be confused with the Common Pheasant.

SUBSPECIES

The Common Pheasant (*Phasianus colchicus*) and the closely related Japanese Green Pheasant (*P. versicolor*) comprise thirty-two and two subspecies respectively. These are separated mainly by the colours of the male's plumage and by geographic isolation. Their natural range extends from the Caucasus, along the Black Sea and east across Asia to Korea, Manchuria, China, Formosa and (for the Green Pheasant) Japan. This natural range has been greatly expanded due to introductions by man and the bird can now be said to be naturalised throughout most of the temperate regions of Europe and North America.

Those subspecies introduced outside their native ranges have freely interbred as have the two different species. No further distinction will be made between the species or subspecies of Common Pheasant, simply referred to as 'the Pheasant' from now on.

MALES AND FEMALES

Pheasants are fairly large birds, typical males weighing around 1200 grams (2 pounds 10 ounces) and the females some 200 grams (7 ounces) less. The sexes also differ in their plumages. The males typically sport a bronze plumage marked with black, a dark metallic blue head and a long, barred tail. They also have bright

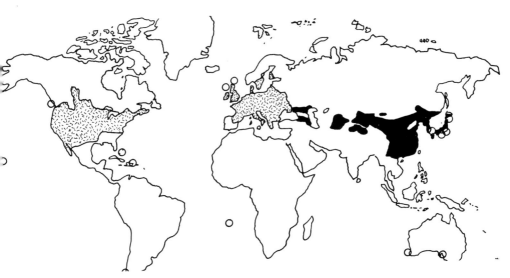

1. *The natural and introduced range of the Pheasant. Black areas = native range; hatching = introduced range; circles = other sites of successful introduction.*

red erectile wattles around each eye and tufts of feathers behind each ear known as 'pinnae'. The females are drab in comparison, with a fairly uniform light brown plumage, a shorter tail and no wattles or pinnae.

This description is of typical birds. Many different subspecies have been introduced to Britain along with strains specially bred by game farmers. The range of colours now varies from black or dark chocolate-brown throughout to pure white. Many birds display a white neck ring of variable extent and white shoulders or wings. Interbreeding of different groups has led to a complete mixture of different features and birds with the plumages of the original population, known as 'Old English Blacknecks', can still be found only in certain areas.

THE PHEASANT IN HISTORY

The first record of an introduction comes from Greek mythology. Jason and his Argonauts were reputed to have brought the Pheasant back from the valley of the river Phasis in the Colchis region of Georgia after their search for the Golden Fleece. These early origins are immortalised in the Pheasant's scientific name, *Phasianus colchicus*.

There is some evidence for the presence of the Pheasant in Britain during the occupation by the Romans, who left recipes and pictures of what may be pheasants in mosaics. They probably kept pheasants as cage birds for the table but there is no real evidence of a wild pheasant population until after the Norman conquest. The earliest certain picture of this bird in Britain comes from the Sherborne Missal at the end of the fourteenth century.

Pheasants were breeding in the wild during the late fifteenth century, and Henry VIII made taking their eggs a crime punishable by a year's imprisonment. They reached Scotland and Ireland in the next century and Wales shortly thereafter. By the beginning of the nineteenth century they were firmly established throughout Britain and their current range covers the whole country, with the exception of the Scottish Highlands and offshore islands.

The Pheasant is probably best known as a gamebird and it is extensively reared all over Britain to increase the numbers available for shooting. However, it should not be regarded as a purely artificial part of the countryside. There are extensive wild pheasant populations, especially in the south-east, and, if man were to cease managing them, they would certainly remain a common bird, although at a rather lower density.

Pheasants are most often associated with cereal-growing farmland, interspersed with small woodlands and hedges. However, they also reach high densities in the Fenlands of East Anglia, where they find cover in the weedy ditches and dykes.

Mating

TERRITORY

Spring brings the countryside to life and pheasants begin to prepare for the breeding season. After spending the winter in the shelter and safety of the woods, the cocks start to set up their territories. This begins in February and is usually complete by the end of March. Competition for territories is intense and not all succeed. In most populations a proportion of the younger and smaller males fail to gain a breeding site and remain non-territorial.

Those males who are successful lay claim to an area along the edge of a wood where it borders on to open ground.

These are typically between 1 and 5 ha (2½ and 12½ acres) in extent. The male displays his ownership by crowing and defends his ground against intruders.

All males, both territorial and non-territorial, will make crowing noises at almost any time of the year but it is only breeding males on their territories that manage the full-blown 'kok-kok' call that is characteristic of this species. This is most often heard at dawn and dusk and is followed by a deep wing drum which can only be heard at close quarters. The call probably has a number of functions: to advertise a male's ownership of a territory; to deter intruders; to attract new hens and communicate to his own harem. Each male has a distinctive style of call; with practice each can be identified from his crow and it is probable that pheasants can recognise each other in this way.

If another male intrudes on a territory he is confronted by an escalating series of displays. First of all the territory owner walks towards the intruder with head and tail held high; if this is not enough he may run towards him. If the intruder stands his ground the resident starts a 'lateral strut', tilting his tail towards his rival and dropping one wing to make himself seem as large as possible. As a last resort the birds will fight: these can be violent and long-winded affairs lasting for up to an hour.

Territorial males display a number of features lacking in their non-territorial counterparts. The red wattles surrounding their eyes can be inflated to cover the side of their face completely; their ear tufts are also erected. While non-territorial birds display both features to a lesser extent, they never approach the size attained by territory owners.

2. *Heads of non-territorial (left) and territorial (right) cock pheasants showing enlargement of the wattles and erectile pinnae.*

3. *A Satyr Tragopan (Tragopan satyra), one of the most colourful members of the pheasant family.*

4. *The head of a Golden Pheasant, one of the two pheasant species apart from the Common Pheasant breeding in Britain.*

HAREMS

By April, most (but not all) of the territorial cocks will have attracted a harem of hens. Pheasants are one of the few British birds with a polygynous breeding system, where one male breeds with a number of different females in the same year. Not only is this unusual in Britain, but the precise breeding strategy used by pheasants, known as 'territorial harem defence', is the rarest breeding strategy of any bird, shared with only a handful of other species worldwide. In Britain the Pheasant is the only bird that breeds in this way.

A territorial male can attract up to a dozen hens to come and reside in his territory at once. The male then guards them as they feed in the open in preparation for nesting. At this time of year the hens graze on growing plant shoots and must feed undisturbed if they are to gain the most energy from their food. The male's role is to ensure that they can fill their crops as quickly as possible without the risk of predation or interference from other males and that they do not waste energy trying to avoid these dangers. A male can just as efficiently guard a number of hens as one, as food and nest sites are not limiting and he contributes nothing towards nest building, incubation or rearing the chicks, so one male can attract a large number of hens to breed with him without any decrease in the help he can give each. As the females are interested only in choosing a male who can effectively guard them whilst they feed, many hens breed with the same male.

Territorial males do not find matters as easy as this may suggest. A small number of males finally breed with the vast majority of the females, but most of the others fail to mate. Furthermore, a male who is successful has to protect his hens from regular invasions by other birds who will try to rape the hens while he is distracted. Breeding males must spend most of their time alert for danger and be ready to fight to protect their harem.

The average harem size in Britain is around two hens, although some males can attract a dozen. In countries where only the males are hunted, the average harem size can be as much as ten. Males have no difficulty servicing this number of females. Experiments with penned birds have raised the sex ratio to 50:1 without any loss in fertility.

When an unfamiliar female approaches a male he walks directly towards her and starts a display very similar to the 'lateral strut' described earlier. He spreads his tail and lowers one wing to make himself seem as large as possible. In many cases he runs along beside the hen or in circles around her. Throughout this procedure the hen usually sits, feeds or looks generally unconcerned.

Once a hen has joined a harem she feeds in a group with the other females and will solicit mating from the male by squatting in front of him. Females usually only allow their particular territorial male to mate with them, although other males will, if given the chance, try to force violent matings on them without any preliminary displays.

From this point on the male plays no further role in breeding. Once she has been fertilised and accumulated enough energy from feeding, the hen moves away from the male and begins egg laying. Although she spends most of her time immediately prior to nesting within the male's territory, she usually lays her eggs outside this area. When off the nest the hen will often return to the male to feed, as she will if she loses the nest.

Eggs, chicks and agriculture

NESTS

Once the male has fertilised the female he usually plays no further part in making the nest or rearing the chicks, duties which fall completely to the hen.

A pheasant nest rarely consists of more than scrapes on the ground. There is no nest lining or arrangement of twigs to give it substance. Although pheasants are typically ground-nesting birds, their nests have been recorded in a range of different locations: on top of walls, in holes in trees and in old squirrel dreys. These, however, are exceptional. Most nests are started in April and, although odd eggs can be found as early as January, these are rarely incubated. Early nests are usually laid on the edges of woods or in hedgerows as crops provide little cover at this time of year.

Hens which lose their first nests can re-lay up to a further three times. These later nests are usually placed in cereal or silage fields. A hen which successfully hatches a brood of chicks and sees them through the first weeks of life will not re-lay: each hen will rear only one brood of chicks per season.

Pheasant nests can contain anything between two and thirty-two eggs. Early in the season the average nest contains around thirteen eggs, although this declines to nearer nine as the summer progresses. The eggs are also very variable in colour, ranging from dark chocolate-brown, through the more common olive-green, to sky-blue. Each hen tends to lay eggs of a similar colour and shape.

EGG DUMPING

These differences in colour help us understand more about another fascinating aspect of the Pheasant's behaviour: egg dumping. In this, some females lay their own eggs in to other hens' nests. Making eggs consumes relatively little energy while incubating them uses a considerable amount. By dumping their eggs into the nests of others, some hens gain an unfair advantage and produce more chicks at less cost. Many of the larger pheasant nests, especially those containing over fifteen eggs, almost certainly represent the efforts of more than one hen and this can usually be seen by the range of different-coloured eggs. Approximately one nest in twelve is thought to contain dumped eggs.

Pheasants do not restrict egg dumping to the nests of their own species. They regularly take advantage of a whole range of other birds. Grey and Red-Legged Partridges are the most usual hosts. There is a record of one unfortunate Grey Partridge hen being found atop a pile of twelve pheasant eggs and sixteen of her own! Mallard are another common host, although what happens to the

5. *A territorial male pheasant crowing in the spring.*

pheasant chicks when their adopted siblings take to the water remains uncertain. Common Pheasant eggs have also been found in the nests of Woodcock, Corncrake, Gadwall, Lady Amherst's Pheasant and Guinea-fowl.

LAYING AND INCUBATION

Hen pheasants lay approximately two eggs every three days, so a typical clutch of eleven eggs takes around sixteen days to complete. During the laying period the hen does not sit on the eggs, only visiting the nest for brief periods to lay another. Hens are very circumspect when approaching the nest so as not to alert

7

predators. If the hen is disturbed during laying, she will readily abandon the incomplete nest and start anew elsewhere.

As the hen does not sit on the eggs during laying, the embryo does not develop. However, once the last egg has been laid the hen begins to incubate. She does this by sitting on top of the eggs and covering them with her breast feathers to warm them and encourage their development. To aid the transmission of her body heat she loses feathers from her breast and belly to form a brood patch. This bald area is well supplied with blood vessels and efficiently warms the eggs.

Incubation takes between 23 and 27 days, during which time the hen spends approximately 23 hours a day on the nest. During her brief periods away she must feed and defecate before the eggs begin to chill. Many nest predators are sensitive to smell and the hen's digestive system changes during incubation to decrease any scent emission. One consequence of this is that the hen produces exceptionally large droppings, known as 'clockers', during her excursions off the nest, which can act as good indicators of a nesting bird in the general but not immediate vicinity.

While on the nest, hens are very vulnerable to a number of different predators and agricultural activities. Their cryptic plumage gives them some protection, as do the behaviours described above, but a great many nests and their hens are destroyed each year.

The causes of losses during laying are different from those suffered during incubation. During the laying period the eggs are more visible and predators which hunt by sight, such as crows, are more successful. On the other hand, many mammalian predators such as foxes usually hunt by smell and find more nests once the hens are sitting on the eggs. Abandonment is another common cause of loss and is more frequent during laying, when the hen has not invested such a great deal of time and energy in the nest. Lastly, agricultural activities and a variety of other factors, such as flooding, account for the remainder of losses. Amongst farming practices, silage cutting is probably the most detrimental, though its importance is secondary to the effects of predation. It can, however, cause large losses in certain areas. In some parts of the United States where silage fields provide virtually the only nesting cover, as many as a quarter of the nesting hens are killed by farm machinery each year.

Apart from differing causes of loss between the laying and incubation periods, the extent of loss varies considerably. During laying, losses can amount to 9 per cent of nests per day compared to only 3 per cent per day during incubation. Losses also vary substantially between areas. In some, less than 35 per cent of nests may survive to hatch, while in others, particularly those where gamekeepers control predators, this can rise to almost 70 per cent.

CHICKS

If a nest survives these many hazards and reaches the end of incubation, the unhatched chicks begin to call to each other and to the sitting hen, who clucks back. These calls help to strengthen the bond between hens and chicks and ensure that all the chicks hatch at the same time. They slow down the development of the fastest-growing embryos and speed up the sluggards. In this way the entire clutch hatches within a few hours of each other, although about one in ten eggs fails to hatch. The chicks peck around the inside of the egg using a special 'egg tooth' on the end of their bills and eventually push off one end like a cap. The newly hatched chicks are warmed by the hen and soon dry. Within three or four hours the hen and her new brood leave the nest and move off into the wild.

The young chicks do not need to feed immediately; their large bellies contain the remains of the yolk sac which nourished them during their development. However, as this is depleted they begin to search out their own food. The hen does not bring food to her young; she brings them to the food. Choosing an area rich in small insects, she allows the chicks to forage for themselves. For the first week or two of life the chicks cannot keep themselves warm and the hen must periodically brood them to warm them up. During cool, cloudy weather the

6. *A cock pheasant of the black or melanistic strain, specially bred by many game dealers.*

chicks need more attention and can spend less time feeding. Similarly, in these conditions there are often fewer insects, so chicks do best in warm weather.

The hen also keeps watch for approaching danger, to which she can react in a number of different ways. On rare occasions, hen pheasants have been seen giving a 'broken wing' display: feigning injury, they attempt to draw a potential predator away from the chicks. A more common response is to give a short alarm call which causes the chicks to scatter and then crouch. After the danger has passed the hen utters a clucking 'contact' call which draws the dispersed chicks back to her.

The chicks are remarkably independent, able to run and feed themselves as soon as they dry after hatching. Their flying ability is similarly advanced. They begin to grow their wing feathers when only a few days old and are able to make short fluttering flights at two or three weeks. At this stage the chicks lose their fluffy appearance and look like small, scruffy versions of the adult hen; they are then described as poults.

The survival of the chicks varies considerably between different broods. Stu-dies of the diet of young chicks have shown that it is the quantity of insect food available to them during their first ten days of life that is the critical factor affecting their survival. Chicks feeding in areas rich in insects tend to be sedentary and survive well; others, raised in areas where insects are scarce, wander extensively in search of food and relatively few survive. Young chicks feed on large, slow-moving arthropods found near ground level, such as sawfly larvae, heteropterous bugs, ground beetles and spiders. As they grow, they also begin to take an increasing number of plant seeds, particularly grasses.

AGRICULTURE AND SURVIVAL

Many of the insects necessary for good pheasant chick survival either live on the weeds found amongst crops or prey on these weed-living insects. Thus, pheasant chick survival is often highest in the weedier corners of modern farms. However, these areas have become increasingly rare with the drive for more productive agriculture. In the not too distant past crops contained many of these weeds and hence good numbers of pheasant and also partridge chicks.

9

7. *Pheasant chicks survive best in warm, dry summers.*

However, the increasing use of insecticides has reduced insect densities, whilst herbicides have removed the weeds on which the insects feed. Cereal fields can now be inhospitable places for hungry gamebird chicks and their chances of survival have declined.

Although insect and weed-free crops may at first sight seem beneficial from a farmer's point of view, many of the insects that have been removed were those that kept various other insect pests in check. The increased spraying of crops can lead to other pest problems and an increased reliance on further sprays to counter them. This pesticide treadmill is a threat to pheasants and to many of the other animals and plants associated with farms.

After hatch, the average brood size is around ten chicks. However, early losses soon reduce this to an average of four in a good year or as low as one chick in a cold and wet summer. Pheasants lay large clutches and the losses of young birds are correspondingly high. Even after they leave the care of the hen when about ten weeks old they continue to suffer losses. The annual survival of young pheasants is between 20 and 40 per cent; for adults this rises to between 30 and 50 per cent. The average life expectancy for a pheasant is only one year and a bird that reaches three or four years can be considered old. Nevertheless, the longest recorded survival for a pheasant in the wild is a highly exceptional thirteen years.

Winter and woodlands

As crops are cut and the evenings draw in, pheasants begin to move back into their winter quarters in the woodlands. They spend most of the winter months in the warmth and security that these provide.

SEGREGATION OF THE SEXES

Throughout the summer the males loaf in the growing crops in small groups of two or three birds while the females are busy rearing the chicks. Once they move into the woods the sexes still tend to remain segregated. Both young and old males remain relatively solitary throughout the winter. They do not form flocks and tend to space themselves out throughout the available habitat. At this time of year the males are often found in fragmented or less suitable habitats such as hedgerows or small clumps of shrubs. In contrast, the females form fairly stable flocks and remain in the best areas of warm woodland.

One possible reason for the differences in the social behaviour of the sexes at this time of year is the preparation for breeding in the spring. Competition amongst the males for the best territories is intense and the prizes to be gained in terms of mating opportunities are great. Throughout the winter the males assess each other and develop a 'pecking order', deciding where each stands before territory establishment in the spring. The males are mutually intolerant and start to lay claim to suitable breeding places.

The females, on the other hand, do not need to compete with each other to ensure a chance to breed in the spring. They can spend their time in the safety of a flock in the warmest parts of the wood. Winter flocks of females contain a stable core of mainly older females who can usually be found together. There are also some females, usually the younger ones, who drift between different flocks. Whether these restless hens are excluded from flock membership or wander through choice remains uncertain.

WOODLAND FEATURES

Although pheasants spend most of the winter in woodland they are particular as to which woods they use. They appreciate, firstly, a wood with a number of edges, places where the wood borders on to open ground. The preferred edges are sloping and so create a gradual change from open ground to full canopy. Pheasants do not like to move far into a wood and spend most of their time within 50 metres (55 yards) of open ground. Very extensive woods do not, therefore, contain many pheasants as large parts of them are too far away from open ground. The ideal size of wood for pheasants is probably not more than 2 ha (5 acres).

The second feature of a good pheasant wood is a well developed shrub layer. A good growth of vegetation at about 1-2 metres (3-6 feet) high will provide both warmth and cover for the birds; woods rich in this sort of cover contain the highest pheasant densities. Pheasants do not appear to be fussy about the species of shrubs involved. They are equally happy in three to five year old coppiced hazel, thicket-stage coniferous plantations or almost any of the early stages of

8. Small woodlands with well developed, shrubby edges provide the best winter cover for pheasants.

9. *A territorial cock pheasant standing alert while one of his hens feeds.*

10. *The variation in size and colour of pheasant eggs.*

11. *A large pheasant nest.*

12. *Newly hatched pheasant chicks are independent and can feed themselves, although they need the hen for warmth and protection.*

13. *A roost of pheasant poults.*

natural regeneration. However, as all these types of woodland develop, the tree canopies close and shade out the vital shrubby cover. High forest with a fully grown understorey, mature coniferous plantations or any bare-floored woodland is unattractive to this species. Pheasants are very much birds of managed woods where they can find trees at different stages of growth. The patchwork of age categories found in coppiced woodlands can prove to be ideal for them.

Groups of pheasants will return each night to a favoured roost, often easy to spot from the piles of accumulated droppings underneath. These roosts are often small conifers such as Lawson's Cypress or larch, which provide dense shelter and warmth during the long winter nights.

FEEDING IN WINTER

Winter can be a time of food shortage for many birds but pheasants seem to cope without great difficulty. They feed on berries, seeds, tubers and overwintering insects found in the soil and leaf litter. They can scratch up the ground with their powerful legs and dig down to buried roots up to 40 cm (15 inches) underground.

Pheasants are managed over most of Britain and sportsmen provide grain in hoppers or along strawed rides in woodland to ensure a high density of pheasants in their area throughout the winter. In unfed areas pheasants are opportunists, eating everything from roots to small mammals in the winter and concentrating on young shoots, grain and insects during the summer. Food is rarely a limiting factor for this species: they can and will eat almost anything.

If food is ever in short supply for this bird it is during the winter. Cold weather can make available food inaccessible for many species as the ground freezes. In a prolonged cold spell pheasants may retire to their roosting sites and sit it out rather than try to find food. They have been recorded sitting motionless in trees for up to a fortnight without any obvious detriment. Nevertheless, although pheasants can take British winters in their stride, the more severe conditions in the American Midwest, with blizzards at -40C (-40 F) have caused dramatic losses. Furthermore, prolonged snow cover can make them more vulnerable to predation, presumably because they stand out against the snow and are forced to leave tracks.

PREDATORS

In Britain the main predator of the Pheasant is the fox. This is virtually the only mammal capable of taking an adult pheasant, although stoats may take hens from the nest. The Goshawk is an important predator of pheasants in other countries, where it takes smaller birds, especially the hens, in surprise attacks. Predation is the main natural cause of death amongst pheasants; few wild birds die of disease, although a sick bird is obviously more vulnerable to predation.

Man and management

Of all birds, the Pheasant has one of the closest relationships with man. It owes its presence in Britain and throughout the western world to us, it is intensively reared and probably more money is spent on pheasant management than on looking after all our other wild bird species put together. Rough estimates place the private monies spent on game management as ten times that spent by the government on funding nature conservation. However, all this attention is not pure altruism. The Pheasant is Britain's most prominent game species and large numbers are shot each winter.

While it is difficult to assess the statistics on a national basis, the Game Conservancy has monitored the extent of rearing and shooting on hundreds of estates since 1961. Unlike almost all other British game species, the numbers of pheasants shot have steadily risen throughout this period, which reflects increases in the size of the population as a result of extensive hand-rearing.

Each summer, sportsmen release birds into the countryside to increase the numbers available for shooting. Originally these birds derived from eggs collected from wild nests or penned laying stock; they would be placed under broody

14. *In the past many pheasants, or in this case partridges, were reared by bantam hens in small enclosures.*

chickens, which would rear them. However, as demand has increased the methods of rearing have intensified. Nowadays, almost all eggs come from penned laying stock and are hatched in large mechanical incubators. Most chicks are then reared in some form of hut or shed using heat from artificial incubators. When about six weeks old the birds are moved into large pens within woods where they are fed and allowed to disperse into the wild. By the beginning of the shooting season in October, these birds are fully grown and provide a substantial proportion of the annual bag.

Pheasants are fairly sedentary animals and most released birds are shot within 2 km (1¼ miles) of their pen. The extent to which they wander is largely influenced by how well they are fed and normally large quantities of grain are provided in hoppers or along straw-covered rides. From studies of tagged birds we know that on average about 40 per cent of the birds released each summer are shot during the following winter. Many of the rest will have died between release and the start of shooting, although enough survive to increase the size of the following spring's breeding population.

Although many people view the Pheasant as a totally artificial species, only surviving due to protection by man and continuing release of new birds, this is not the case. Many areas in the south and east of Britain contain substantial wild populations which are self-sustaining. Nevertheless, the size of the population is increased by management and if rearing were to cease it is estimated that the population would fall to around 10 per cent of its current level over Britain as a whole.

Despite the role of hand-reared birds in maintaining pheasant numbers at a high level, reared birds suffer a number of handicaps compared to their wild counterparts. Their survival in the wild is

15. Modern game farming involves artificial incubation and rearing large numbers of birds indoors.

16. *The survival rate of hand-reared pheasants is low. Many are taken by predators, like this cock bird killed by a fox.*

consistently lower than for wild birds, as is their breeding success. This is possibly a result of the absence of a parent when they are reared and subsequent poor predator recognition and avoidance, although the details remain unclear. If some way were found to make hand-reared birds as good at avoiding predators as wild ones, then their improved survival and breeding success would probably lead to the population being doubled within a year.

PHEASANT SHOOTING

In a typical day's pheasant shooting in Britain the birds are driven from woods or cover crops by a line of beaters and made to fly over a line of seven or eight standing sportsmen armed with shotguns. Each wood is described as a drive and usually seven or eight separate areas are driven per day. Typically, each wood is driven three times per year although in areas where many birds are released this is increased.

The season extends from the beginning of October until 1st February, but few birds are shot until November, when the leaves are off the trees and the birds fully feathered. Early in the season most estates will shoot both cocks and hens, with only males being shot towards the end to conserve a good stock of females for breeding. As pheasants are polygamous only a small stock of males is needed to ensure that all the hens are fertilised and in the spring they can be shot much more intensively than the females without the risk to the size of the bag in the following year. On purely wild bird estates it is possible to shoot up to 20 per cent of the hens and over 90 per cent of the cocks without endangering the production of young in the summer. On areas where birds are reared these figures become meaningless as extra birds can always be released to compensate for any shortfall caused by heavy shooting.

Pheasant shooting is a popular and lucrative activity, with many consequences for the countryside. A survey of landowners has given pheasant shooting as second only to landscaping as the reason for their planting new woods and retaining existing ones, while the value of sporting rents generated by small woods

17. *The Pheasant is the most numerous gamebird in Britain and is extensively shot during the winter.*

often exceeds the value of the timber they contain. In the face of recent agricultural intensification, pheasant shooting has been one of the few incentives for farmers to manage their land with wildlife in mind; furthermore, it is an incentive with the potential for profit.

Apart from encouraging the retention of diverse features on farms, pheasant shooting also leads to other forms of active management. If woods are to be made attractive to pheasants they must include wind-proof edges, light, sunny conditions inside and rides for feeding and flushing the birds. These conditions are ideal for the many species of wild flowers and butterflies once common when farm woodlands were managed for timber or coppice. However, the decline in small woodland management, resulting from poor markets for the produce, had led to woods being increasingly shady and overgrown. Increasing coniferisation has also played a part in the decline of many species once associated with light, open woods. Pheasant management is one of the few remaining incentives for farmers to open up their woods to the light.

PESTICIDE USE

Increasing use of pesticides to maintain high yields in cereal fields has led to them becoming relatively sterile environments for game and other wildlife. Fungicides, herbicides and insecticides are now routinely sprayed on most fields and remove both the insects and the weeds on which insects feed. Many of the plants and insects killed by these unselective sprays are harmless to the crop but are vital if gamebird chicks are to survive. Once common flowers such as poppies and Corn Marigolds have all but vanished from farms and gamebird chick survival has fallen to levels insufficient to sustain many populations.

Concern for wild game has led landowners to investigate methods of adapting pesticide use to favour gamebirds without detriment to their profits. Experiments by the Game Conservancy's Cereals and Gamebirds Research Project into the more selective use of pesticides around field edges have doubled chick survival. They have also doubled butterfly numbers and led to the return of many species of flowers listed as scarce or rare.

Although government and voluntary conservation bodies can protect areas of special value to wildlife, their power to alter land use more generally is limited. Over most of the countryside the fate of wildlife is in the hands of the landowners. Pheasant shooting provides them with a paying incentive to compromise the aims of intensive agriculture and forestry and is one factor working in favour of a richer and more diverse countryside as a whole.

Studying pheasants

IN THE WILD

Pheasants are common enough for anyone living in lowland Britain to be familiar with them. However, there is a great difference between recognising the occasional bird seen on the roadside and knowing where and when to observe them displaying and interacting.

The most spectacular displays can be seen during March, April and May when the males are on their territories and females breeding out in the open. The best way to see pheasants at this time is to use a car as a mobile hide. Although wary of people, pheasants are fairly unconcerned about cars and can be approached to give superb views through ordinary binoculars. Most activity can be seen during the first two hours after dawn and, to a lesser extent, before dark. There is usually little to be seen during the day when the birds lie up in cover. As described earlier, the males establish their territories along the edges of cover and any shrubby woodland edge bordering a field of winter cereals should provide good opportunities for observation.

Pheasant territories tend to be found in the same places each year, although this

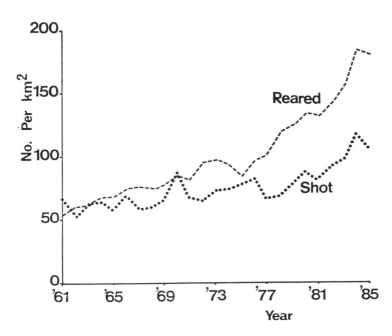

18. *Changes in the number of pheasants reared and shot per square kilometre on shooting estates in Britain since 1961, as recorded by the Game Conservancy's National Game Census.*

19

19 (right). *Numbered back tags allow wild pheasants to be followed individually, a valuable research tool.*

20 (below). *Fitting small back-mounted radio transmitters to hen pheasants enables the collection of detailed data on movements, breeding success and survival.*

does not mean that it is always the same birds that are present. The plumages of male pheasants are sufficiently variable for individuals to be recognised and a thorough knowledge of the birds of a locality can greatly add to the satisfaction and information obtained. If you suspect that there is a territorial male in an area but are unsure, then one option is to set yourself up as his rival. The two syllable 'kok-kok' call of the male is fairly easy to imitate, if rather hard on the throat, and will often elicit a response from the nearest males. Males will often start calling in response to any sharp noise, such as a slammed car door, and some American scientists even used sticks of dynamite to encourage their birds to crow. Cocks will also respond to earth tremors and a sudden burst of calling can forewarn of an imminent earthquake.

During the nesting season the best advice is to leave well alone. Hen pheasants are very sensitive to disturbance during laying and any approach may lead them to abandon their nest. If the nest is unoccupied and the eggs cold, this does not necessarily mean that it is abandoned: it could be that the hen is still laying. These seemingly deserted nests are often the ones most vulnerable to disturbance.

The only reliable method of seeing chicks and poults is from a car on stubbles in the late summer. Hens and their broods are still together at this time and can be readily observed around dawn and dusk as they glean seeds from the fields. Wild birds can be distinguished from their hand-reared counterparts by the presence of an adult hen, their warier nature and sleeker plumage. Newly released birds tend to look rather battered from life in a pen but this disappears as they moult into their adult plumages.

During the winter months there are fewer opportunities to watch pheasants. They spend most of their time in cover and tend to be secretive.

SCIENTIFIC METHODS

Beyond simply observing pheasants in the wild, scientists use a number of other techniques to acquaint themselves with their life and behaviour. One of the best tools is to be able to identify individual animals. As mentioned, many of the cocks can be distinguished by differences in their plumages but hen pheasants present a largely uniform appearance. Numbered tags provide the best solution to this problem: many of the results described here have been ascertained from studying populations of birds fitted with individually marked back tags. Marking with metal leg rings or small wing clips has also provided useful information regarding survival and dispersion although it tells us less about behaviour.

Probably the greatest breakthrough in the study of wild animals has been the development of radiotelemetry; this has revolutionised work on pheasants. In this method, birds are fitted with small radio transmitters: for pheasants this typically consists of a small battery-powered package hung around their necks or fitted to a harness on their backs. This emits a pulsed radio signal on a set frequency. The scientists can then home in on this signal with a directional aerial and special receiver to find the bird in any sort of cover and at any time of day or night. Using this method it is possible to collect very detailed information from individual birds: where they live, what they eat, who they mate with and so on. This tells the scientists much more than they could discover through observation alone.

Although it is always preferable to gain information from wild birds living free in the countryside, there is also much to be learned from the examination of dead birds. Pheasant shoots provide an ideal opportunity to examine large numbers at a time of year when they are otherwise hard to study. This can provide details of body weight, health, diet and age.

AGING PHEASANTS

Accurately aging pheasants is a complicated procedure, although there are many features which can give a rough guide. Once pheasants have grown their adult plumages, there is no way to separate young from old by sight; this requires closer examination. Young cock birds tend to have smaller, rounded spurs on their legs compared to the long, sharp spurs of adults. While this can be an effective way of separating the age groups

21. *Radio-marked pheasants can be located in any kind of habitat and at any time of day through use of a directional aerial fitted to a small receiver.*

22. *Collecting tags from dead birds after shoots can give valuable information on survival.*

in the autumn and early winter, it is not entirely reliable, especially by the late winter when the spurs of the young birds have finished growing.

Another technique for aging dead birds is to look for the Bursa of Fabricius, a small vent inside the cloaca that is only present in young birds. Although this is a very effective method, it requires some practice and is only suitable for aging dead birds.

Probably the best method for the scien-tist is to measure the width of the base of the tenth primary wing feather. As young birds develop their adult plumage when only half-grown, their feathers tend to be shorter and narrower than those of adults. Measuring the diameter of this feather at the point where the first barbules develop enables most birds to be separated into either adults or juveniles. Adult birds have shaft diameters of over 3.1 mm (0.12 inch); males below this diameter are juveniles as are females with

23. *A hen pheasant with her well grown brood feeding on stubbles in the autumn.*

measurements of less than 2.8 mm (0.11 inch). Females between 3.1 mm and 2.8 mm (0.12 and 0.11 inch) cannot be accurately separated into adults or juveniles. These values can vary between different areas and are only a rough indication. As yet there is no way of separating different age categories of older birds.

In conclusion, studies of the Pheasant have revealed much of its life history and found it to be an adaptable and successful addition to the British avifauna. Much work has been initiated owing to interest in the Pheasant as a sporting bird and management for shooting ensures that the species will remain a prominent part of country life in the future.

Further reading

Delacour, J. *Pheasants of the World.* World Pheasant Association and Saiga, second edition 1977.
Hill, D. A., and Robertson, P. A. *The Pheasant: Ecology, Management and Conservation.* Blackwell's Scientific Press, 1988.
Johnsgard, P. A. *Pheasants of the World.* Oxford University Press, 1986.
McCall, I. *Your Shoot: Gamekeeping and Management.* A. and C. Black, 1985.

ACKNOWLEDGEMENTS
   Photographs are acknowledged as follows: T. H. Blank, 5, 15, 23; D. A. Hill, 11, 16, 20; K. C. R. Howman, 4; J. Marchington, 22; I. McCall, 17; M. C. Swan 13. Other photographs, including the cover, and the line illustrations are by the author.